I Wish I Knew

By

Evelyn Asante

ISBN 978-1-7332210-0-9

Preface/ Preamble

Reflecting on my pre-teen years until now, I wish I had known so many things. I wish I had known about the experiences of others to caution, encourage, and strengthen me. I wish I had made different choices.

The following are a series of interviews from some people willing to share their experiences. I pray that whoever reads this book will benefit immensely and be proud of who they are as individuals, as well as appreciate the love and support their loved ones are offering. I hope they acknowledge what others have gone through so that they do not repeat similar mistakes.

Though most the instances are true, the names have been altered for confidentiality. Other circumstances are written as observed.

Content

Introduction

It is, indeed, very true that time flies! It feels like it was just four days ago when, at the age of thirteen, my parents were doing their best to guide my choices regarding friends, education, being closer to God, and relationships with boys.

At the age of twelve, most children feel they are grown since they are almost teenagers. As they start to gain another level of independence and identity, some transitions from preteen to adolescence are seamless, while others are messier/more challenging/tattered. Children may think their parents are too controlling and old-fashioned. They may think they know better than their parents. The sad part is that, by the time one realizes that their parents were right all along, sometimes there has already been a lot of pain and broken hearts with actions that cannot be undone, no matter the regrets.

Individual Life Experiences

Lavell:

Being a preteen was rough as I had body issues. I had a big chest and never fit in. I tried to find the group that I fit into and could not, so I joined the gang and failed terribly. I also always felt like I was on the outskirts because of my intelligence. There was a lot of uncertainty. I tried to mold myself to be someone that other people would like, forgetting "me" and trying to please others.

As I became a teenager, I got over trying to fit in and molded a spot for myself. I volunteered at the park district and found like-minded individuals. This caused a shift in my family dynamics because I saw this group of friends I had found to be, in my opinion, like family. Unfortunately, my mom did not agree; she always warned me not be around people who latched onto me or used me. I never saw her point until I was older.

My twenties were filled with many things I thought I knew, but they were falling apart in front of me: things like friendships, love, and figuring out who I really was. Around the age of 21, I realized I didn't know who I was. This was because I was dating a lady at that time. I devoted all my time and energy into the relationship. When it fell apart, I realized I had nothing! Not even knowledge of who I was. So, the rest of my 20's was devoted to defining who I was going to be. It was full of mistakes.

If I could do it again, I would be more decisive in my choices. In most of my life, I have adapted to life as it came. I will be more prudent in choosing the path that I want to walk as I pay attention to what my mother tells me.

Tobias:

I wish I could have let my head lead me, whilst I was in love, rather than only my heart when making decisions. Though my wife and I have a great relationship, we both wish we could have taken it just a little slower. Now Julie is 21 and I am 23. We are struggling to take care of our little princess, Ellie, whilst we are both in school.

There are times when you just don't know what you were thinking when you did stuff, and it is too late to turn back the clock to correct yourself. The most painful thing in life is had I known. Truthfully, what can you do with that? What good is it to wish you had done things differently? It is more troubling when you had loved ones who gave lots of caution, but they were all either ignored in disrespect or flatly rejected.

I met Julie when I was in my third year in college and she was in her second. We were inseparable. When I told my parents I wanted to take our relationship to the next step, my parents begged me to take it a little slower and at least finish my first degree. All that fell on deaf ears and thinking I was grown and had the right to do whatever I wanted to do. We went ahead and got married at the court.

In no time, Julie was pregnant. We were so excited, but we realized we were in school. We had to look for an apartment near the school while preparing for the baby. I had to work extra hard to provide for my family. Julie tried her best to help, but she was not feeling very well most of the time.

Instead of just relaxing during the summer vacation, I had to work two jobs. Doctor appointments were becoming more frequent. It was now getting to me. How did I grow up so suddenly with all these responsibilities? I was becoming so tired. I wished I could just relax, work just one job, and re-energize for the upcoming academic year. There was no time for that.

If a relationship is until death do us part, why rush? I wish I could have waited to finish my master's degree and start a job. We could have had a big wedding. Well, it's not like that now. Instead, I could have studied intensely and hurried with school. Our parents are supportive but we both did a lot of damage with disrespect just to get our way. They were right after all.

James:

I remember like it was a few days ago: around the age of seven years, when my mother had a restaurant and my dad worked hard to take care of me and my siblings. I helped my mother in any way I could whenever she asked. In the country that I grew in, we had a two-bedroom house with seven people living in it.

My older brother and I slept on the floor, but we were still very happy because we had each other to play with. I was never disrespectful to my parents. I listened to their advice. I was fortunate enough to come to the United States at the age of twelve. As I became a teenager, my parents frequently talked to me about school. We were not that rich so education was my only was to a better life.

During my adolescent years, I finished high school and attended two years of college. Unfortunately, my mother was still in Haiti, and my dad remarried. It was not easy. I had to take care of myself and my younger brother.

As young as I was, I worked full-time, sent my mother money, and paid rent as well as the difference of my college fees. Though my stepmother was a pharmacist, and my father worked for the steel mill, they were not willing to support me financially. I was not allowed in class till the remaining amount was paid in full. I also had to rent my parents' car whenever I wanted to use it. That was when I gave up on school.

Working at Walgreens, I was paid only $5.75 an hour in the photo department. That was not enough for all the expenses I had to pay.

Though I was respectful at home, it was not easy. I could not eat in the house because my step-mother said she was not willing to cook for a grown man. After my eighteenth birthday, my dad put out brochures of the Army, Air Force, and Navy on my bed. This made me very sad because I knew the implication. I started making plans to move out.

Now in my forties, I am married with two beautiful teenage daughters and have been working in a warehouse. I promised myself not to have another woman and to do the best that I can for my wife and children.

With all that I know now and knowing that I was not going to finish college, I would have learned a skill or worked two jobs to save money just to go and spend more time with my precious mother. Nobody can ever replace her.

Ronelle:

I started growing a little taller and realized my growth was not stunted as my siblings had been teasing me. Having four sisters and a brother, being the youngest of six was fun as they did most of the house chores. The down side was that someone was always telling you what to do. Eventually, my moustache and goatee grew in. I gained a little weight. I was the man! I wanted to be left alone and spent a lot of time with my friends.

My parents loved me so much and told me several times to take my education more seriously. They were ready to pay all the expenses. They said that was the only inheritance they could give me that would truly be with me no matter where I went. Regrettably, it all fell on deaf ears. This constant advice and my rebellion made me find excuses to spend more time out of the house as I was not getting along very well with my brother and sisters either.

My older sisters got married and left the house, as did my older brother. My parents were still encouraging me to find solid ground in education. I acted very little on that. At this time, I was making some money as a computer technician, but my parents still made most of the house expenses. I used my money on myself!

The highest education I received was high school. I also completed a short course in computer software. That was the best that I did whilst I had the support.

My Christian life was also a joke. I neither went to church nor read my bible.

Now, I am married with three children. I have a lot of responsibilities and the money is not enough! How I wish I had listened to my parents.

I feel like a big fool. I feel like I was played. The friends that I hung out with, and that I clearly remember we all decided not to do our assignments, are now doctors; a lawyer and another is a business owner.

I still wonder when they decided to do all their assignments and get so far ahead.

Did they hate me that much? I thought we were very good friends. In some instances, I put them ahead of my family.

I sometimes wake up at dawn and ask myself how all this happened?

Now, both parents are dead. My other siblings help me a lot, but they all have their own responsibilities. If only I had drawn closer to God, I would have listened to my parents' advice and made better choices.

If I could do it all over again, I would make my parents very happy by studying as it would benefit my future. I would be doing better than a technician with no proper certificate. I would have listened to by brother and sisters and appreciated all the help they offered me. I would have loved my parents more. I do not even dream about them. I really miss them so, so much.

Rebecca:

At the age of twelve, one of my nipples started becoming just a little bigger. At the age of thirteen, the other also started developing. I was so uncomfortable and shy. I felt very uneasy, but my mom encouraged me that it signified the beginning of adolescence. It was a must to take a shower twice a day and take time for myself rather than just playing with my older brother as I used to. At the age of sixteen, in high school, I met a final year student as I started eighth grade. My parents were very much against it, but I had no plans to stop seeing Liam.

My rebellion brought a lot of tension in the house. I felt like an outsider in my own home, which I did to myself. I could see the worry on my parents' faces, but unfortunately, that did not stop me. I spent more time with my friends and, sometimes, my boyfriend. One Friday evening, after I had spent some time with my boyfriend in the park, he dropped me off at home. He said he was going to do his laundry and watch a movie at home.

At about nine o'clock, I felt bored at home. Since the weather was nice, I walked almost seven blocks to his house to surprise him. To my utmost surprise, there was another lady from our school sitting on his couch with him. He had his hand around her neck. I froze! Then, I saw them hug. He turned and saw me, ran to me, said he was sorry and could explain. I was speechless. I guess I put my trust in a man, and he failed me. My parents were right! I hated to admit it, but it was true.

I could not manage school the next day and had the privilege of spending the day with my dear mother. I could not hide it from her. She was so comforting. She reminded me of how young I was and that I was not ready to commit to marriage. She reminded me of all the opportunities in life and told me to decide on what I wanted to be in future. I listened half-heartedly because I was really hurt, but she prayed with me and reminded me to trust God. I said "Hi" to him and that was the most we said to each other. I did not need any explanation. What I saw that evening was enough.

I spent more time with my family and got very involved at church. Though a lot of young men wanted to date me, I was not ready for any of that. I could not let myself be that hurt again. I felt I was not ready neither did they sound ready to commit. I found a lot of peace in just focusing on my goals in life till I finished college and met a handsome man who was ready to fully commit. I asked him a string of questions. We courted for two years to pray and study each other.

We have been married for six years now. We do not always agree but we respect the uniqueness of our different opinions. I always thank

God for my parents and their patience for me. I still appreciate them so much especially as I have my own children now.

Annabelle:

I thank God for being my guide during my teen years. I was very involved at church. There was always good supervision, so there was no time to do anything bad. I was a very strong-willed, young girl, spoiled by my grandma and much loved by my dad. It was different with my mother. She did not understand nor accept my views. This made our relationship a little strained at times, but I still loved her dearly.

My siblings and I had our moments. There were peaceful times. Other times it was just chaos. We agreed to disagree; each of us just kept what we believed in. In a way, it really helped me as a grown woman because I am not easily swayed. I always insisted on what I wanted or believed in and made sure I got what I wanted my way. Though I listened to my parents, I always thought I was right. We sometimes had family meetings and hearings when my parents saw that a disagreement was lingering.

I did my best in school as my parents advised with proverbs 15:20 in mind. "A child who brought tears to the parents is a fool." My excellent relationship with God helped me tremendously by protecting me from making mistakes and by making better choices that pleased the Lord. I first had a boyfriend when I was twenty years old. My mom was flatly against it. In a way, she was right because the relationship did not last; but her motive was not legitimate since her only reason was because he was under privileged.

I am now married with two handsome boys and with few regrets. The one thing I wish I could really do differently was to convince my dad to let me pursue science subjects. He convinced me to switch subjects, and I ended up with business management. Though I'm using it to manage my insurance business, I still have the passion to be in the medical field. I know it is never too late, so now I am going back to my first love. This way, I can be in a lab as I have always dreamed.

I guess I could have convinced my dad more. In all, I thank God for the life of my parents and siblings. Now we all have families of our own, and I wish we fought less and just patiently talked it out. We still have our differences, but we handle them very well now. When we are together, no misunderstanding between us lasts more than an hour. My dad has passed, and we all realize we do not have the time to waste and fight. Rather we focus on loving each other.

Vanessa:

We are just two girls of my mother. My mother told us our father passed when we were babies. She always said she would never remarry so she could take good care of us without distraction. I could just tell my mom really missed her husband and resorted to prayer and singing. What a dedicated mother she was and a wonderful grandmother our children are blessed to have.

The daily and weekly routine was very strict with no deviations or excuses. It was as if we were in a Catholic boarding school. We were just two years apart. Our washrooms were cleaned twice a week on Saturdays and Wednesdays at six o'clock at night as my mother supervised us. We had discussions on personal hygiene at three o'clock in the afternoons on Sundays and off-the-record talks afterwards which we loved so much.

Off-the-record meetings started when my sister and I were twelve and fourteen years respectively. We talked about body hygiene, respect for our bodies, and relationships including peer pressure, embracing who we are as individuals, and a lot more. These talks really helped me build my self-esteem. I was not worried to be alone. We had a sheet of our personal expectations and the stumbling blocks we might face. It was very practical and achievable.

With all this priceless guidance, my sister and I were sometimes just tired of the hovering of mother. Now, with the little life experiences that I have had, I had a surprise fiftieth birthday party for my mom that was dedicated to thanking her for the unrelenting support and guidance. I sometimes felt I was too suppressed, but I truly cannot blame her. She told us all of what she knew.

Times are gradually changing as I sometimes imagine. My grandma used firewood in her mud house to cook and, after a while, graduated to coal pot. She refused to use gas. Just imagine being told that if you sang while taking a shower, your parents would die, only to find the real reason was to prevent soap from getting into your mouth.

Another myth that I remember so well was my grandma insisting you never sweep after dark because it would make you poor. My mom believed it too. It was recently when we talked about it that my grandma admitted that the real reason was to prevent sweeping away a valuable. This was because, in those times, there were no lights, but lanterns.

Oh, we laughed and told Grama Mary to tell us all her little tricks. She, in the mist of laughter, said it was for our protection.

Abigail:

At the age of sixteen, the power struggle was intense. I felt like my mother opposed me on everything I did, especially my dressing, and I did not like that at all. I still did it anyway and was grounded most of the time.

I tried to dress like my older sisters, and they normally told me I was unique, so I had to dress differently to suite my stature. I just did not get it. We are five girls, and I was the youngest. My sisters were petite, and I was very tall. They were all between five-one and five-three. I was six- two! And very well built. I just loved makeup, very long nails, long hair and bright colored dresses.

My dad did not want me to feel limited because of my stature, but my mother was very strong on my dressing and outlook. I thought my mom did not like me, and so we were not that close, though my dad tried to explain to me that she had my best interests at heart.

After the Christmas holidays, my mother told us she will be going to Ghana to visit our grandparents during summer and will stay for two months. My parents were from the same town in the central region of Ghana. I was happy to see my grandparents, so I quickly told her I would go and live with my grandparents. My parents agreed to it, and I was really looking forward to the trip. I talked to all four of my grandparents and decided to spend a month at each home. It was just about seven blocks apart as my parents described.

Summer eventually arrived and I did not leave any of my favorite dresses behind nor did my makeup. I was very excited to live with my grandparents for a change. The flight was peaceful as my mother, I guess, decided not to talk about my dressing anymore.

At Kotoka International Airport, Accra, in the capital of Ghana, I could feel the stirs. Wow! She is from America! I heard someone whisper. Guess what I was wearing? A purple long wig, a red croup top, and a bright light green long shirt with a slit almost to my thigh, red high heels, and a big red handbag. I now really felt so sorry for my mom. She never said a word. I guess she was praying all that time for a miracle of change in me from God.

My older sisters decided to go with my mom to her parents' house. It was very warm, so I mostly wore shorts and tank tops until Sunday morning arrived. Both families decided to go to church together, and so my mom was to come with my other sister, so we all go since the church was closer to us. All four of my grandparents, my sisters, and mom were waiting for me. I was the last to come out of my room.

Once I got to the living room, like it was rehearsed, both of my grandmothers asked where I was going with that dressing and makeup? Then turned to my mother and said they were disappointed in her that she could not help me dress well and allowed me to look like that. Then they asked me how long I have been dressing like that. I felt so bad for my mother. I knew she had tried so much to help me. I literally had no say. My sisters and grandfathers including my mother went to church. My grandmothers and I stayed home. There was a CLEAN UP! Then a lecture followed. I was in Ghana!!!! No escape! No talking back! No choices!

Grama Elsie was my mom's mom. She was a fashion designer. Though old, she was still very fashionable. SHE made me take off my fake eyelashes, cut down my long nails, and wash my face; and my grama Anita gave me her dress to wear. It was nice. It was a light purple straight dress to my knee. I was as tall as my grandma, so it fitted me well. I felt like I was in a trance. What did I get myself into?? I just had no say. They did not ask my opinion about anything.

The program for the day all changed because of me. I accompanied them to the kitchen to prepare lunch. The original plan was to go to a restaurant was postponed to the following week.

The talk of my dressing was suspended for the rest of the afternoon till my mom, sisters and grandparents left, then my Dad's mom grama Anita told me to go to bed a little early because she needed my help on a project.

I woke up about four o'clock in the morning and heard that she was already up, so I joined her. On the big dining table, she had a pile of pieces of materials, a sketch pad, and other accessories. I knew she did now sew but why all those pieces of material? I kept that question to myself. I never knew Grama Else also came to spend the night.

We prayed, had tea, and I guess they tried to be very nice to me and in a low tone; they both express their surprise of my outfit on Sunday morning. Grama Else said she had a wedding coming up and needed ideas of the dresses she had to make for the bride since she entrusted everything to her. The lady in question was six-one; I was just a little taller than her.

In about three minutes, Grama was able to sketch a lady like her, and then she cut some material for us to see how it would look on her. She also had her picture. Those two old ladies really set me up. I was the one saying the colors were too bright, the nails were too long and suggested just a little makeup will look very nice on her.

As we were still working, Grandpa brought some fried eggs, bread, porridge, Ghana doughnuts, and I really enjoyed it. It was almost eleven o'clock.

Grama Else saved all the suggestions and the lady arrived at about twelve-thirty. She was very pleased with the recommendations.

After she left, then there was the question: "Do you now realize how people will see you with what you tried to wear, and that you really need to listen to your mother if she suggests? We believe she has tried. True or false?"

In a low tone I answered, "Yes."

They told me how beautiful I was and so there was no need to try that hard or prove it to nobody.

Though I still want to stand out when I dress, I always consider the occasion and it makes a lot of difference.

Interestingly, I am now married with almost three teen girls and a boy, I started having the "small private" talks with them both. But I have ONE just like me. My mirror. She is really sticking it to me. I am surprised my parents had all that patience for me and the embarrassment I caused them.

I'm so blessed to have my mother. I took her to a special lunch, and we talked about my teenage years. We cried and laughed, and I apologized.

Just do it right as you read this. You can have all the fun you want and still make your parents happy.

Miguel:

During my freshman year, my parents talked at length to me about friends at school and the choices I made. It was not just that, they were also very strict. I had a nice cell phone, but it was very restricted.

The Wi-Fi in the house was turned off by nine o'clock because my siblings and I normally had homework to do. I can say they were trying their best to make sure I was safe and a good example to my younger brothers since I was the oldest. I joined football and track. My *loving* mother was always there before practice or game was over. That was if she was not there the whole time to watch the game. She said she just enjoyed watching me play.

In all their efforts, the unappreciative son still found ways and means to do the unthinkable. Thank God they never found out. I guess I would have been homeschooled after that. With the help of some of my friends, I was able to vape, use the pen, and then actually smoke marijuana. It was just a couple of times each. I felt I got away with it.

My parents often told me, "You know we are doing our best, remember any wrong thing might be on your record. You are just beginning life; you cannot mess up your future." And all talks ended with, "Remember God is watching." That made me feel guilty, but I was still anticipating on a next time that I could try again.

I tell you, it is good to listen to the news sometimes if not often. It is not just for our parents. I was watching the news recently when they started talking about vaping. I paid a little more attention.

According to the Centers for Disease Control and Prevention (CDC), more individuals who vape were reporting having seizures. There was a nut in my stomach, why look for sickness when I am healthy? I have seen someone with seizures, and it was not good. I cannot go looking for embarrassment like that.

During that weekend, I told my mom I wanted to go to the library. She wanted to go too. So we spent about three hours there. I did my research, and I decided never to touch any drug again. I read on the CDC website that tobacco use is the leading source of avoidable disease, sickness, and death in the United States. I had to get a plan and a story to tell my friends. It really terrified me. Make time and go to that website and read it for yourself. It is reliable information. There is so much information. I am blessed to be healthy.

I started talking to myself. I had to decide. After learning all that, my future was in my hands. I did not want to have Chronic Obstructive Pulmonary Disease commonly known as COPD and be on multiple medications. COPD is a group of diseases that cause airflow blockage and breathing-related problems. It includes emphysema, chronic bronchitis" it is mostly caused by smoking. If it is avoidable why go look for it? I asked myself. There was no need to lie about it.

I told my friends to read about it and bluntly told them I was not ready to be sick like that. Two of my friends also stopped. Their exact words were, "This is crazy. Buy sickness? No. we can start saving that money towards college. We still have a lot of fun without drugs."

We study to get good scores in our SAT. We sometimes do a spelling bee, and that is the most fun as well as writing words with twenty-five letters in two minutes. Try it yourself. Other productive ways we are spending our time is learning instruments. Collectively, we have drums, flute, saxophone, keyboard and bass guitar. We are doing it. It is fun and peaceful.

Think about the things you are doing that you think you have gotten away with, try to know more about them. How will they impact your future? I was glad I was listening to the news that day.

I have still not told my parents, especially my mother. I might after college. There is no need to let her worry when the problem has been solved already.

Frank:

Age twelve was not that bad. I was still very close to my mom and helped her a lot. Then I tasted the little left over from my dad's beer. I liked it. Having Christ in a home and in your personal life makes an enormous difference.

At the age of thirteen, I was drinking. I was sharing with my dad without his knowledge. Though I was not drinking much at that time, that was how it all started. At the age of seventeen, I could not control it very well. I could not go about my normal duties without being a little tipsy and made sure I had a bottle or two of beer before going to bed.

Most of the time I kept to myself and felt my parents were always against me in everything I did. I guess my mom sensed something was off, but since I mostly tried to avoid her, she did not know I was drinking, and my dad did not realize that I was helping him drink his beer.

We were just two children of my parents. My younger sister was nine, and I was seventeen at that time. Since I secluded myself and acted grown up, my sister got all the attention from my parents. The home usually felt empty though we were all at home. Most of the time my dad was busy on the computer, and my mom with my little sister.

It was just boring for me, and my grades also started to suffer since I took no delight in studying until we went to a mini vacation for my cousin's wedding. We spent a week at their house. They were a Christian family and had morning devotions for twenty minutes starting at quarter to six. They sang, read the Bible, and prayed. Every morning, each person said what they were thankful for. It was so different for me and by the fourth day, I liked it. I could not have beer either.

My cousin Andrea always said she was grateful for her parents' guidance and support. On the day of the wedding, the pastor preached about love and the need to cherish each other because if even we had a thousand years, it will still come to an end.

Things became better after that time, and I stopped drinking as my supplier also stopped drinking. We all tried to go to church on Sundays and on Saturdays. We had Bible devotions promptly at nine o'clock at night. It was good.

Now after twenty-eight years, I am married with three children. My son is twelve and is already having those moody days. I try to be interested in all that he does. Either I like it or not; it's just to be close to him.

Unfortunately, my mother had stroke and is in a nursing home. The stroke was a little severe, so her speech is slurred. Though she is alive, I really miss my mom. I miss how active she was, jovial and always cleaning. Now she must be helped in doing so many things. I wish the clock could turn back. I would love them more, respect her even more, and help in the house as much as I could. I realized how hard it was for them, but they never complained.

After work, I am so tired, but I still come home to take my kids to their activities and check the mail to note the bills coming in. Sometimes, it is just overwhelming. My dad and I are best bodies now. I took the time to appreciate and thank them for all that they did for me, especially their patience. I truly hope all of you reading this will get the chance to admire your parents!!

Maame Nhyira:

Preteen was fun because I was the youngest child and the only girl. I had three older brothers. I guess I was the miracle baby because the gap between me and my brother was eight years, but the older ones were all two years apart.

At the age of eleven, taking a shower twice a day was the norm. No matter how my day was, I still had to have my twice-a-day bath. Thirteen was still fun because being the only girl, I was always with either my parents or one of my brothers. I would not say I was spoilt, but none of my brothers ever bothered me. One of them was always on my side to defend me, and it was good.

Rules in the house were discussed before they were in place, and so there were no excuses. Family Bible study time was seven o'clock at night on Saturdays, and it was fun because, at the end, my dad always read a chapter in proverbs as a reminder of what God expects from us.

As in Proverbs 1:10 says "A wise son brings joy to his father, but a foolish son brings grief to his mother." We sometimes discussed our actions, and another was always praying that "the words of our mouth and the meditations of our heart be acceptable to God." In Psalm 19:14. This has always been my guide in life and has really helped me. I have no problem saying this verse over a hundred times in a day and meditating on it.

I did not always have my way, especially at the age of sixteen when I wanted to hang out more with my friends. A school function was allowed but nothing more, or my mom was our chaperone at the age of sixteen. I just could not believe she did that. I had a lot of guys asking me to be their girlfriend, but I had heard enough, and I knew I was not ready for a relationship and neither were they in high school. I felt it was a distraction, but I had friends of both genders, and we normally hung out in my house, and that was OK with my parents.

My father and brothers treated me with a lot of respect, though. I was the youngest, and they always reminded me that anybody who did not treat me with respect was not fit for my love. My self-esteem was very high, and I really thank my parents and brothers. Just embrace the love of your parents and siblings. It will not last forever. At age thirty-one, I have my doctorate in psychology. The truth was that, it was not as easy as you might think I had it. I listened to advice and knew I could make it. You can make it too.

My family is very proud of me and I am happy I made it. This is the least we can do for our parents. Make them proud.

Dorothy:

I had been moving from one foster home to another and, at the age of twelve, just when I thought I had a stable life with my foster parents for two years, there came another move. I was sad and tired of the uncertainties. This home that I went to was in a nice neighborhood.

That Friday evening, as the case worker and I arrived, it was dinner time and they were waiting for me. The house was very clean, and everything was very well organized as I was stealing glances at the surroundings of my new home. The two adults talked for a few minutes.

"Dorothy, this is your new home and your new guardian, be good and I will be in touch. Mrs. Andrews, please meet Dorothy and thank you for your help."

I smiled but was choking with tears. Mrs. Andrew led me to my room upstairs to put my suitcase down and told me to join them for dinner. My room was big with a queen size bed. It was nicely decorated. This was the first time I have had such a nice room to sleep, but I knew all the other foster parents tried their best.

There were two girls and a boy, all teenagers, and it looked like I was the youngest. Mrs. Andrews introduced me to them, and Stella prayed before we ate. It seemed she knew she was supposed to because once she finished talking, she said, "Let's bless our food." There was very little talking during dinner time but once we were all done, she formally introduced me to the family and mentioned all their names and told me they had a schedule which is supposed to be followed.

We all got along very well because there was no room to talkback anyway, and the expectations were very clear. It was a Christian home and very orderly. They were all ready to help each other, and we all had chores to do, and it changed every week on Saturday at eleven o'clock in the morning after we were all done with our weekend chores.

Mrs. Andrews was a great mother figure because she was very fair. I got to know later that the oldest girl (Abigail) was her only child and nothing showed because she treated us all the same. Education was a priority to her. She made sure we all asked our teachers for extra credit assignments and expected nothing less than an A. She had the time to support all of us with any help we needed and getting in trouble was or having a detention was prohibited, although we were allowed to defend ourselves when it was needed. She made sure we all did what we were supposed to do. She would knock and the next second, she was in your room.

I am now married with three children and still get in touch. Mrs. Andrew has spent two Christmas holidays with me and my family. I am forever grateful to her. I thought she was too strict, but she really helped me to be a good wife and mother. My home is always clean, and I have a schedule that I try to keep because my children are young and in training.

God has always been my strength whenever I felt all was lost. Being in a Christian home really helped me to learn that God is our strength and hope, an ever-present help in times of need. The word of God has been a light unto my feet. Though God has blessed me with a good life, I still wish my parents were alive. There is nothing like a perfect life. Just appreciate your parents and ask for God's grace and strength for them. You are privileged to have parents if yours are alive!

Ryder:

I am very protective of my family because I was an orphan at age fourteen. So, I was very aware of a parent's love and all the other people who try to genuinely love you, but it is never the same. I was not a problem child for my parents, but I thought I had all the time. I never dreamt that I will lose both parents within two years.

My mom's younger sister took my two sisters and me in. She was a good mother to us. I could see she did all that she could to console us. She treated us just like she did her own kids, but i just missed my mother terribly. How did it happen so fast?? All that was left were memories. It was just a very bad accident. A driver lost control and drove straight into a store where my mom was shopping. It was a big shock. It would have been a little different if she was even sick for a while.

"Bye mom, bye my dear Ryder, see you in the evening. I will prepare your favorite meal for dinner" was the last thing we talked about. My dad had passed two years ago from cancer, and the family was just recovering from our loss because we were very close.

Our parents try but remember we are not perfect. Cherish every moment and count your blessing each day. I know it could be better, and it could be worse sometimes. I discipline my children when I must, but I love them like it is my last day with them. I guess I have never recovered from my loss.

Riccardo:

It had almost been two weeks, and my mother was still talking about my grades and my attitude towards my studies. Truthfully, I knew and believed I was doing my best. I guess it was not good enough for her and that really made me feel a little stressed out and disheartened. I did not even feel that hungry.

My dad, thankfully, realized that my demeanor had changed and not eating as usual, and I guess was worried. On June twenty-four, which was a Saturday, check your calendar, and you will find the year. That was not too long ago.

My dad told me to get ready. He wanted us to take the car to the washing bay and do some detail cleaning on the car. He teased me that I will be driving soon, and my apprenticeship had just started. Though a bit relieved, I thought he might continue the talk, because they were a great team and always agreed and supported each other. It took us about two hours to finish cleaning the car, and we headed to IHOP which he knew was my favorite place. Thankfully, he never mentioned school, so I was relaxed and enjoyed the breakfast.

He really caught me off guard. "How are you doing in school"? He finally asked when I least expected the question.

My first response was, "You, too?"

He quickly came just a little closer and said, "I am not judging you. Let's talk and it ends right here, I promise."

I relaxed a little and told him I believe school is not my thing. Math makes me dizzy, and you find it everywhere.

"At least I know simple math that can get me by," I said.

The next question was, "So what are your plans and what do you want to do after high school?"

My dream and fantasy are to be a mailman. I have admired them ever since I was in elementary school. One thing I know I am good at is remembering addresses. I have no problem with that, Dad," I said.

He sat quietly as I talked for over thirty minutes. He just listened. He smiled and said, "We have to convince your mother. It is OK if you do not want to go to college. What's most important is good management and truthfulness in life."

He was so surprised I had done all this research and never shared it. I knew not going to college was not an option. I was surprised by his response that we needed to convince Mom.

My dad then said, "Unfortunately, you took after me," then he smiled.

He explained that, he is a hands-on person and so, after attaining his associates in industrial maintenance technology, he decided not to further his education. Now, as the head of maintenance in a school district, he is enjoying his job with good income as my mother the bookworm is a pediatrician.

This is what life is about he said, to accept and respect each other and all the differences. My parents love and respect each other, and their levels of education have never been a subject.

"Please help me convince mom to end my education after high school". I said.

"Don't worry," he said. "It will be OK.

I gave him a hug and felt so relieved for that outing. The other thing I had to do was some money management classes at church. I said yes, with a smile. At dinner the next day, my mom gave me a look and said, "Your dad told me your concerns. Just do your best and finish with good grades."

I said a big, "Thank you" to both. It was a great evening for me with a heavy burden lifted.

PS: June 24, (2017) was a Saturday**

Ike:

Ike was my best friends' teenage son who was just a little spoilt.

I truly did not recognize him when I went to visit him at his aunt's house.

This was not the story of Cinderella but very similar. Ike, Alanna's only child. She was not dead but in a mental hospital. Alanna married her high school sweetheart at the age of eighteen and had Ike early in life.

"It was like waking up from a very bad dream, that became a reality and taunted me," as Ike narrated to his mom's best friend.

"My aunt Stacie has a big hardware store about a mile and a half from the house. She lives in a beautiful house with her three boys and a little girl. She had taken over my mom's store too when she became sick. I was treated like part of the family the first week I moved to Auntie Stacie's house and soon the reality set in".

"I became the house boy. Instead of being served, I was serving. A couple of times, I had to sleep in the garage because my job was not satisfactory. She refused to take me to visit my mother and that broke my heart. My mom will think I have forgotten about her, but I have not. I wish I could see her to hug her, apologize and express my appreciation for all that she tried to do for me which was never enough for me."

"Thank you for looking for me and finding me in this village," my mom's friend said with tears in her eyes.

It has not been easy, I replied. "I had to save every penny I had and started asking around because Auntie Stacie will not tell me anything,"

"I learned she was at Ankaful Psychiatric Hospital in the central region of Ghana, in West Africa. Once I had that information, I started planning my trip in detail. From Accra to Cape Coast was a long journey and, as a house boy who interacted with other kids normally on errands, it was easy to have someone who knew the place to gave me some direction."

"Fortunately, Amos had plans of going to that area, so I waited and tagged along and that was a great help. He took me to his house, and the next day accompanied me to the hospital. Seeing my mother for the first time was very tough and emotional."

"I saw my mom and she was so happy to see me. She is not as crazy as it was described to me. I was doing some manual labor for the man (Amos) so I can stay for free to be able to visit her daily. What I hated most was cleaning the hencoop which was big. Hens laying on eggs wanted to peck me. It was so stinky. It has not been that easy.

We talked every day, and I begged one of the nurses and convinced her that my mom was better and thanked her. She observed and realized that too. My mom was taken to a different department and this nurse, I guess, was an angel sent just for my mom and me. It was very improved there. There were only two people to a room and a little spacious than the crowded rooms with more than ten patients.

"It all started when my dad decided to move out due to some *personal* reasons as he put it. It was so sudden my mom did not take it too well.

"Her world came to an end. She did not shower, ate very little, talked to herself all the time, and was mad at everybody. She was dragged off when she started hitting and throwing anything her hands laid on. "

"Don't worry, I will take it from here," Auntie Alanna said with tears in her eyes. "I will find a temporary apartment and do all I can to make sure she is well, and we can all leave."

"I hugged her so tight and sobbed. I could see some light at the end of the tunnel. I was so happy to see my mom's friend. It is true that difficult times reveal your true friends. My mother and I had many friends but in those tough times, they all vanished into thin air except for Auntie Stacie and the new friends I had developed as a nobody.

"There was so much hope now. She started talking to me about me going back to school. I was so grateful. There was no talking back as I used to. I could sleep through the night. My mother was doing so well the doctors had an anticipated date of discharge. I took a lot for granted but I learned the very hard way how fortunate I was.

"You cannot do it all in a day but do the best you can and appreciate the efforts others are making for you. I am grateful to God for giving me another chance with my mother."

Timothy:

I am not ashamed to say that I was from a poor home. I mean extremely in need. That's what I saw growing up. My friends had enough, but my family was always in need. In some instances, my father had to borrow money for food. Some of our neighbors were very nice, and I guess just wanted to help so if they ever sent any of us kids on an errand, they would give us money or food.

Though our parents never warned us, we never wanted charity like that. It was sad and tough. I wondered how they started, but I could not ask that question. Though we were deprived, we were a very tight knit family.

We talked about it sometimes, and my parents always encouraged us to study hard and save the family from the situation. My dad went to burn wood, and my mom sold the charcoal. She also sold dried fish, chewing sticks, and sometimes cassava. Most of the time the food stuffs being sold ended up in our tummies. We did not have much, but we were very happy, and our parents encouraged us to be honest in our dealing and trust God. Two girls and two boys during our teen years was fun as well as a lot of restrictions especially in dealing with the opposite sex.

They explained to us that we should keep our virginity till marriage. As my dad explained, "If you impregnated a girl, where was she and the baby going to sleep?" There were more probing questions like, "Are you ready for the lifelong commitment when you are in school? Rather, start praying for God to help you all to make the right choices when you are ready."

My youngest brother had a girlfriend after all that talk, and my dad whipped the lust and love out of him. We laugh about it now that we are adults, but it was not the least funny at that time. It did not end there; my parents went to have a talk with the girls' parents too. That incident put a lot of fear in the rest of us and to the glory of God, we are all very successful. They were both illiterates and really encouraged us. I sometimes taught my dad how to read. Our self-esteem was very high as my father always reminded us that if you did not steal or tell lies that someone can use to embarrass you, we were OK.

We all took our studies very seriously, and we have two doctors, a pharmacist and an accountant. God blessed us so much. Our parents are still alive though old. Their job is to spend time with their grandchildren, and we provide them with all they ever wish for. Glory to God!!!!!

Ponder Over These....

As much as we all try, life is not seamless as we all wish so let us be very grateful for the parents and guardians we have and make the best out of every moment.

I truly and sincerely wish I could have a second chance. Though I was helpful at home, I would have done more. I have a deep appreciation for my parents now that I have my own children.

A few of the things children take for granted that parents go through;

- The sleepless nights when you have babies or have a child not feeling well
- Planning meals daily so there is variety for the family
- Keeping up with the cleaning of the house
- Doing the unending laundry;

I am blessed to have washing machines, but I clearly remember like it was a few days ago that every weekend there were heaps of laundry that my mom did. From morning till sometimes afternoon, she would break to serve lunch and then continue.

- Asking for money ……. there was never the thought of whether they had it or not. I was very unhappy when I did not get all that I wanted especially whenever school was reopening. The question was; why don't you have it??

Thinking my dad just did not want to give it to me.

I never thought about all the bills and other minor expenses.

It is OK to ask your parents how much they make and all the expenses they have. This will help you appreciate them very much. They are making enormous sacrifices that are never spoken.

What is your goal in life?

How can you make it achievable?

What are some of the things that can prevent you from attaining it?

What changes do you have to make to be on track?

Do the people around you discourage or encourage and respect your goals?

It is sometimes OK if you are not people's favorite because you do not blindly follow them.

Believe in yourself!!!

54

Prayer

Mighty God, thank you for our parents and guardians.

Thank you for the strength you have given them to take care of their children though it is sometimes not easy.

Continue to grant them wisdom, courage, good health, and long life.

I pray that children will be obedient to their parents and lead lives that are pleasing to Your Name Lord.

I pray for wisdom as they take their studies seriously so that they will excel as this is the prayer and wish of every parent.

Help us to make the right choices in life.

I pray that children will not die before their time and parents will live to see their children's children

In Jesus' Name.

Colossians 3:20 "Children, obey your parents in everything, for this pleases the Lord."

Conclusion

I thank God for the opportunity He has given me to put this script together. It is my fervent prayer that we will all find peace in every situation that we find ourselves in and cherish each other. The prudent person listens to advice. It goes a long way to make our lives better. If only I knew what I know now, I would have made a lot of different choices. I will also acknowledging every advice as a privilege and taking it very seriously. All my parents wanted was to make sure I had a good future. It is not a bad thing to have friends, but it is very important to have a scale of preference and a priority list with set goals in mind.

It can be recognized that we all have our share of regrets in life, but the unfortunate part is that we had somebody to caution us. This could be our teachers, parents, or leaders in various organizations; but if we still have breath, there is still the chance to make things right and make the best choices because the most painful thing is to live with regrets.

What situation do you find yourself in now? Are you making the best choices in life? Are you trying to blame somebody else or have you already placed blame? It might not be the best or what you wish for; but count your blessings and make the best out of every situation. Is there a lesson you can take from it? Maybe it will strengthen you and be a testimony to encourage others.

Below, you can write your original goals and where you are now. Are there any deviations? Set new ones or adjust the previous one that you had.

About the author

Evelyn Asante always desired to be an author and has just made it real by her first book.

She has a bachelor's degree in psychology.

Evelyn has a passion for the youth and young adults which led to this book. She recollects her days as a teenager: the peer pressure, love and advice from her parents and the reality as she is a parent now.

Taking a moment to stop and listen and be of assistance is what she loves to do.